THE HARBOR
AT SCITUATE, MASSACHUSETTS

HARVEY H. PRATT
FOR

A.W. George, M.D., *President*
Frederic T. Bailey, *Vice-President*
W. Marriot Welch, *Secretary*
George F. Welch, *Treasurer*
Charles H. Waterman
Max M. Alder
Richard Wherrity
Walter Haynes
Francis Harrigan
George F. Dwyer } *Directors*
Eugene Buckley
Harvey H. Pratt
George H. Newton

Scituate Harbor Improvement Committee

THE SCITUATE HISTORICAL SOCIETY

ISBN: 978-0-991090923-2-1
Copyright © Scituate Historical Society 2014

Digitally Reproduced in 2005 by:

CDR CONVERPAGE
23 Acorn Street
Scituate, MA 02066
781-378-1996

www.converpage.com

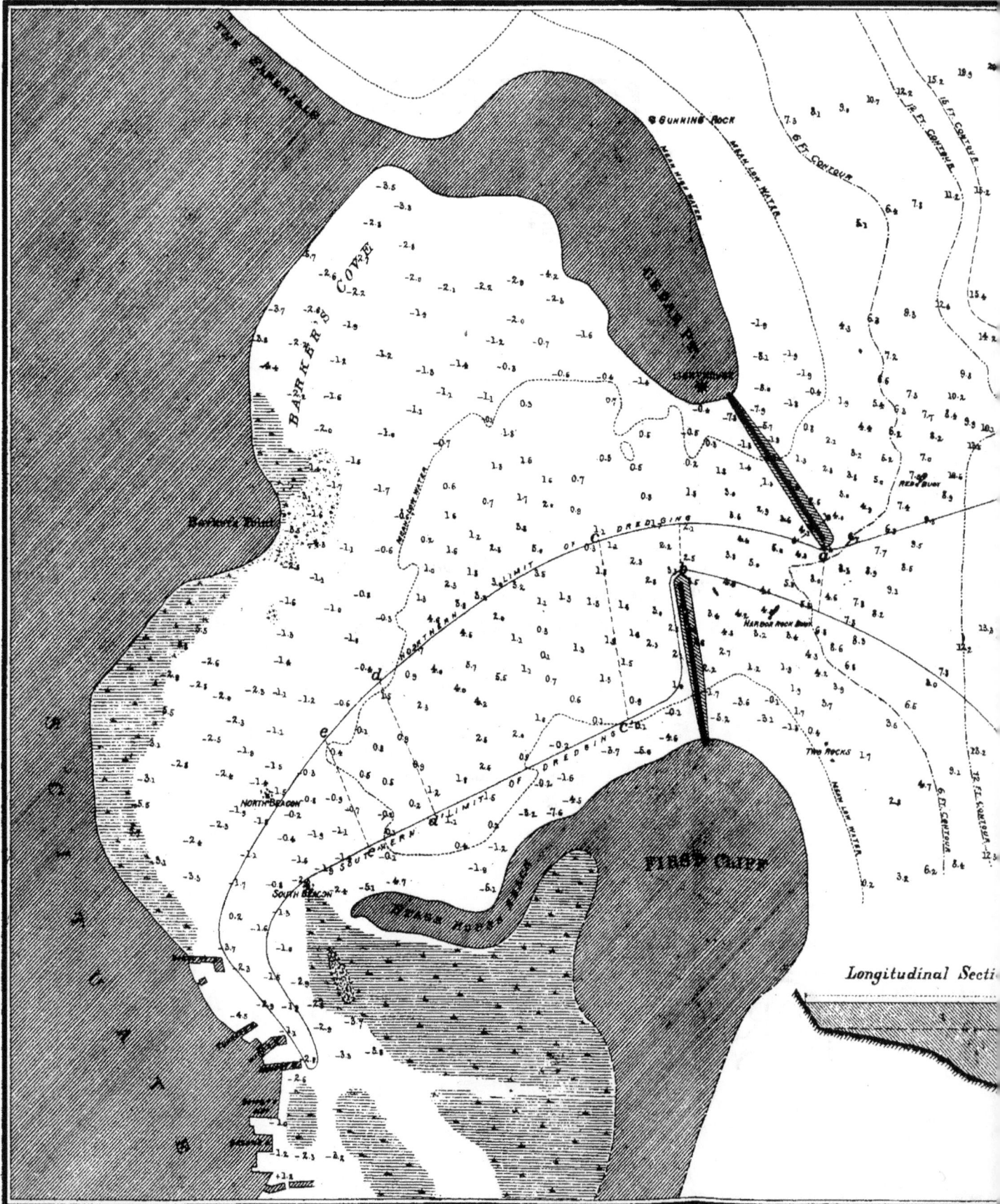

Longitudinal Section

MAP OF
SCITUATE HARBOR MASSACHUSETTS
SHOWING THE PLAN ADOPTED
FOR MAKING IT A HARBOR OF REFUGE
Projected by
BVT. BRIG. GENERAL GEO. THOM, COLONEL OF ENGINEERS.

Scale of Feet

The soundings are expressed in feet and tenths and are referred to the plane of mean low water.
The mean rise and fall of tides is about 9¼ feet.
The project adopted for deepening the harbor and the entrance thereto consists of excavating
it, within the limits shown on the drawing, - as follows
1, Outside the extremity (a) of the northern breakwater, to a depth of 16 ft. at mean low water.
2, Between (b) southern " and (a) to a depth of 12-16 ft at m.l.w.
3, Between southern breakwater and line c-c' to a depth of 12 ft at m l w.
4, Between lines c-c' and d-d' to a depth of 10 ft. at m.l.w.
5, Between lines d-d' and e-e' to a depth of 10-3 ft at m.l.w.
6, Between lines e-e' and the wharf front, to a depth of 3 ft at mean low water.

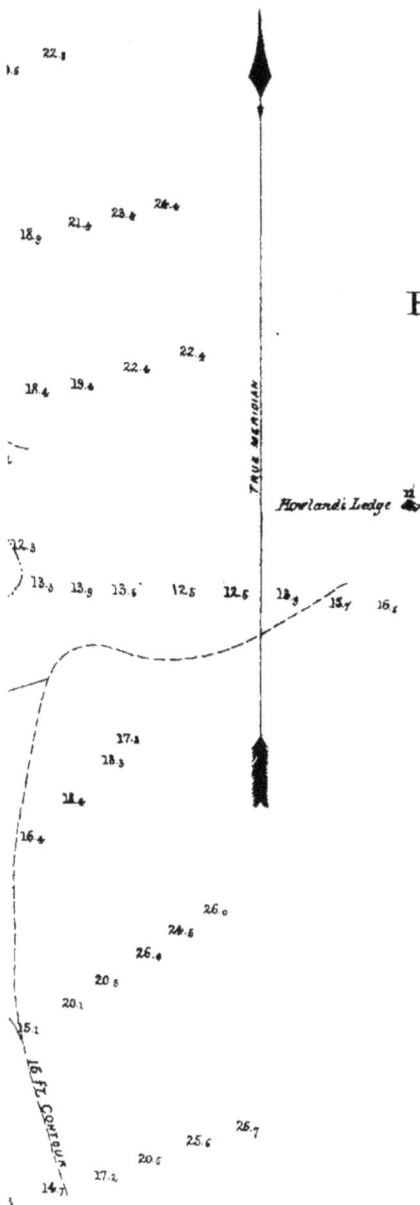

Howland's Ledge

16 ft. CONTOUR

TRUE MERIDIAN

Section on Line a-b.

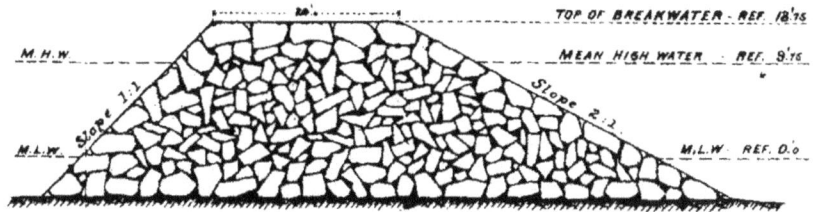

TOP OF BREAKWATER - REF. 12.75
M.H.W.   MEAN HIGH WATER - REF. 9.75
Slope 1:1   Slope 2:1
M.L.W.   M.L.W. REF. 0.0

...on of Breakwater off Cedar Pt.   Long. Section of Breakwater off First Cliff Point.

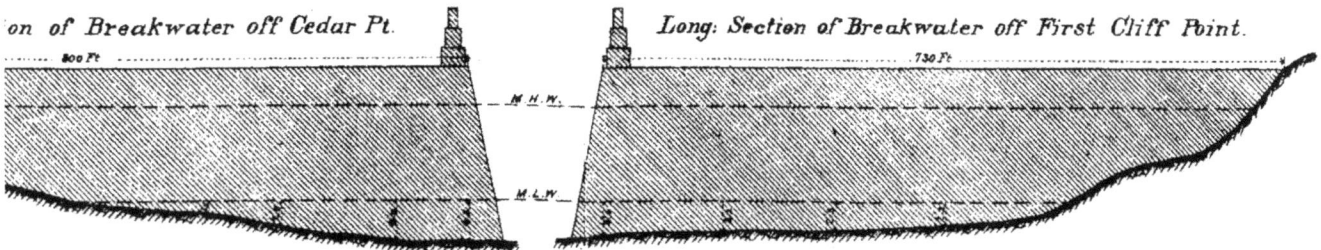

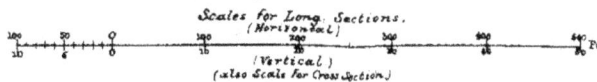

800 Ft   730 Ft
M.H.W.
M.L.W.

Scales for Long. Sections.
(Horizontal)
(Vertical)
(also Scale for Cross Section.)

THE HARBOR
AT SCITUATE, MASSACHUSETTS

BRIEF ON BEHALF OF ITS IMPORTANCE AS A
HARBOR OF REFUGE AND AS A
COMMERCIAL PORT

I.

SCITUATE AS A HARBOR OF REFUGE

Scituate is geographically situated farther to the eastward than any other point on the Massachusetts coast between Cape Ann and Cape Cod. Its shore is rocky, treacherous and forbidding. Its coastwise line of about eight miles in extent has been the scene of many marine disasters in the last half century.

A correct list of wrecks that have occurred on this shore from 1807 to the present year follows:

1807	Ship Cordelia, built at South Scituate on the North River. Captain Dorr. On her return voyage from China. In 1890 a piece of her timber could be seen wedged in between the rocks of the ledge.
Feb. 1, 1831.	Schooner Edward, probably from Bucksport, Me. Went ashore one mile west of Scituate Light.
Feb. 17, 1844.	Brig Bordeaux. New Orleans to Boston. Captain Sage. Went ashore on Long Beach.
May, 1844.	Schooner, name unrecorded. Ashore on Long Beach.
Jan. 20, 1845.	Barque Marine. Wrecked on Cedar Point.
Oct. 1845.	Schooner, name unrecorded. Wrecked on the Third Cliff.
Nov. 25, 1846.	Schooner Sidney. Wrecked on the Third Cliff.
Nov. 25, 1846.	An hermaphrodite brig, name unrecorded. Wrecked on the Glades.
Dec. 17, 1846.	Brig, name unrecorded. Wrecked on Gull Ledge.
Feb. 17, 1847.	Ship Dublin. Ashore on Long Beach.
Mar. 29, 1847.	Brig Maria. Ashore on the "Hummock" beach.
Nov. 25, 1847.	Ship Alabama. Liverpool for Boston. Struck on Minot's Ledge. Sunk three miles east of the ledge.

Jan.   1848. Barque Natchez. Wrecked on Marshfield (now Huma-rock) beach.

Mar. 10, 1848. Barque Frances Barr. Palermo for Boston. Captain Tailor. Wrecked on the Fourth Cliff.

May 22, 1848. Ship Ocean Monarch. Wrecked on the Second Cliff.

May 31, 1848. Ship Scot. New Orleans for Boston. Struck in Bassing Cove.

Nov.   5, 1848. Brig Siroc. Captain Stimson. Struck on Cedar Point.

Feb. 18, 1849. Brig Oscar. Captain Wilson. Wrecked on Tilden's Point.

Feb. 18, 1849. Ship Jennie Lynde. Ashore on Long Beach.

April 16, 1851. Brig William. Cadiz for Boston. Wrecked at Fourth Cliff.

April 16, 1851. Brig Elizabeth. Matanzas for Boston. Wrecked at mouth of the North River.

April 16, 1851. Schooner from Thomaston, Me., laden with lime. Ashore at the mouth of the North River. Burned. This was the storm that carried away the lighthouse on Minot's Ledge.

Sept. 21, 1851. Brig Partridge. Wrecked on the Third Cliff.

Sept. 21, 1851. Barque. Name unrecorded. Wrecked on Gull Ledge.

Sept. 21, 1851. Brig. Name unrecorded. Struck on Bar Rock.

Feb. 29, 1853. Barque Forest Queen. London to Boston. Forty emigrants on board. Wrecked on Second Cliff.

Mar.   2, 1853. Schooner. Name unrecorded. Wrecked on Third Cliff·

Dec. 29, 1853. Schooner Mary E. Pierce of Bangor. Wilmington for Boston, ashore at North Scituate.

Dec. 29, 1853. Brig Clio. Savannah for Boston. Wrecked at Fourth Cliff.

Dec. 29, 1853. Schooner Mt. Vernon. Ashore on Cedar Point.

Dec. 29, 1853. Two schooners. Names unrecorded. Ashore on Marsh-field beach.

Dec. 29, 1853. Packet barque Maryland of and for Boston from Balti-more. Ashore inside the Glades. Mrs. Turner notes here that "The heavy gale and snow storm of December 29 was disastrous to shipping on the New England coast, especially in the vicinity of Cape Cod, where nearly an hundred vessels have met with more or less disasters attended with considerable loss of life."

Jan.   1854. Barque. Name unrecorded, ashore on Marshfield beach.

Dec.   3, 1854. Brig T. P. Perkins of Portland. Wrecked on the Fourth Cliff.

Dec.   3, 1854. Schooner. Name unrecorded. Wrecked at the mouth of the North River.

Dec.   3, 1854. Brig Lafayette. Wrecked on Gunning Point.

Jan. 19, 1855. Scotch brig Elizabeth. Wrecked on Third Cliff.

Feb.   4, 1855. Schooner Northern Light. Ashore on Tilden's Point.

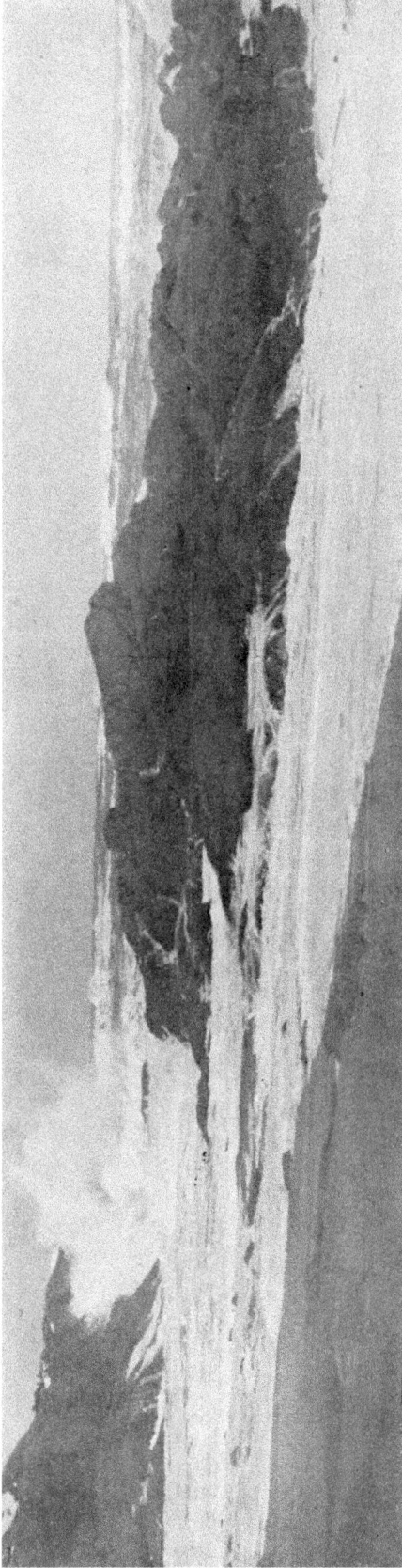

Ledges off North Scituate, two miles from proposed harbor of refuge.

Wreck of barge Kohinoor off North Scituate March 3, 1916.   Five lives lost.

Wreck of barge Ashland off North Scituate March 3, 1916.

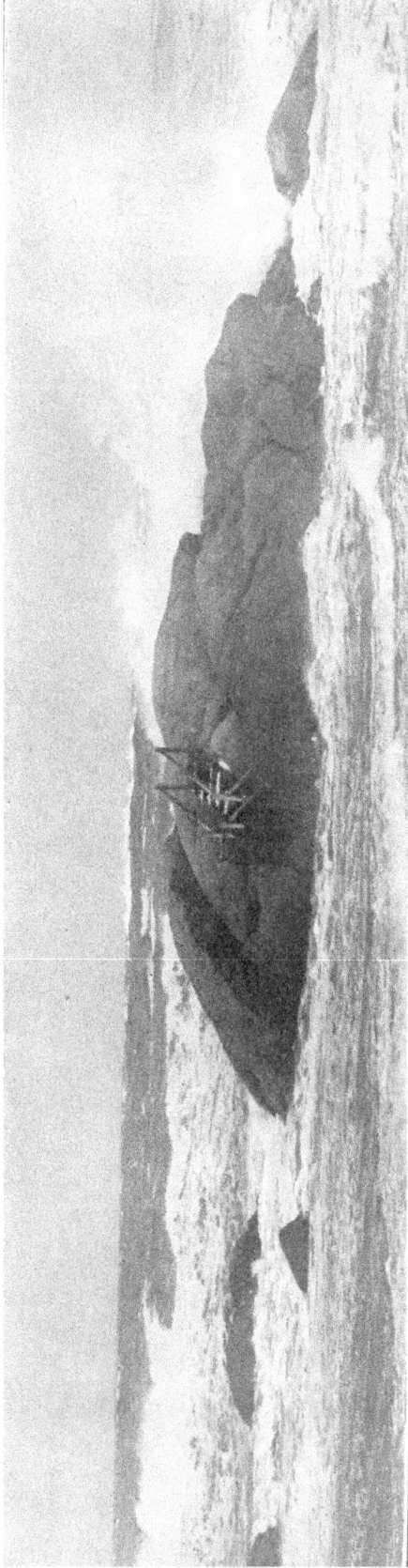

"Well Rock," North Scituate near Mike's Ledge.

Mar.   10, 1855. Ship. Name unrecorded. Wrecked on Fourth Cliff.

Mar.   10, 1855. Brig. Name unrecorded. Ashore on Fourth Cliff.

Nov.   29. 1856. Brig Moro. New London for Boston. Ashore on First Cliff.

Jan.   18, 1857. Brig Judge Hathaway. Captain Small. Wrecked on First Cliff.

Jan.   19, 1857. Schooner Geneva. Georgetown for Boston. Captain Perry. Wrecked at the "Drain."

Dec.   22, 1858. Schooner Sally Badger. Pittston, Me., for New Bedford. Wrecked at the "Charity House."

Jan.   27, 1859. Ship Roebuck. New Orleans for Boston. Wrecked on the "Willies."

Feb.   26, 1859. Ship Elizabeth. New Orleans for Boston. Wrecked on Cedar Point.

       1861. A schooner. Name unrecorded. Wrecked on Minot's Ledge.

Mar.   1861. Vessel. Name unrecorded. Wrecked on Jenkins' Ledge.

Mar.   1861. Ship. Name unrecorded. Ashore on Cliff beach.

Nov.   7, 1862. Schooner Maine Law. Ashore in Barker's Cove.

Dec.   6, 1862. Schooner. Name unrecorded. Ashore on Gunning Point.

April 1863. Schooner Ruth. Wrecked on Ellm's Beach.

Nov.   1866. Schooner. Name unrecorded. Wrecked on Deacon Litchfield's Point.

Jan.   1, 1868. Brig Julia Lingley from Peru. Ashore on Long Beach.

Mar.   1868. Schooner N. E. Clark. Charleston for Boston. Wrecked on the Glades.

Dec.   1, 1868. Schooner. Name unrecorded. Wrecked on Fourth Cliff beach near the Charity House.

Mar.   1869. Schooner. Name unrecorded. Ashore on Long Ledge.

       1871. Schooner. Name unrecorded. Wrecked near the harbor.

       1873. Barque. Name unrecorded. Wrecked on the Hazards.

       1873. Schooner. Name unrecorded. Wrecked on the First Cliff.

Jan.   29, 1875. Schooner Maracaibo. Ashore on Gunning Point.

Jan.   30, 1875. British Schooner Bessie. Ashore at the mouth of the North River.

April 1884. Schooner Martha Weeks, laden with lime. Ashore by the Turner Meadow drain. Burned.

June   28, 1885. Schooner Elsie Fay. Rum Bay, B. I., for Boston. Ashore at Cedar Point.

June   28, 1885. British Brig Hotspur. Barbadoes for Boston. Ashore on Smith's Ledge, Egypt Beach.

Jan.   9, 1886. Schooner Joel Cook. Captain Springer. Of and from Philadelphia for Boston. Wrecked on Third Cliff.

Jan.   9, 1886 Schooner Isaac Carriten. Ashore on Humarock Beach.

4

Feb. 3, 1886 Schooner Mary A. Kellen. Havana for Boston. Wrecked on Third Cliff.

Dec. 7, 1886. Schooner Florence A. Q., Lunenberg, N. S., for Providence. Wrecked on beach one mile north of Cedar Point.

Dec. 7, 1886. Brig Susie Kiffen. Captain George Kiffen. St. Johns, N. F. for New York. Wrecked on beach one mile north of Cedar Point.

May 27, 1887. Schooner June Bright. Captain Barter. Ashore on Egypt Beach.

Feb. 10, 1888. Schooner Agnes R. Bacon. New York for Boston. Wrecked near the Fourth Cliff.

June 25, 1888. Barque Chattanooga. Porto Rico for Boston. Wrecked at the mouth of the North River.

Nov. 25, 1888. Schooner Edward Norton. Wrecked on First Cliff.

Nov. 26, 1888. Schooner J. Lock. Captain Isaac Banks. Boston for Yarmouth, N. S. Wrecked on Turner's Beach.

Jan. 7, 1889. Schooner W. Parnell O'Hara. Ashore on Second Cliff.
Mar. 5, 1889. Brig T. Remick. Surinam for Boston. Captain Fossett. Wrecked on North Scituate Beach near Life Saving Station.

Mar. 6, 1890. Steamship De Ruyter. Antwerp for Boston. Captain Arfsten. Ashore on Gunning Point.

Feb. 13, 1894. Schooner Minnie Rowan. Baltimore for Boston. Wrecked on Second Cliff.

Feb. 15, 1906. Steamship Devonian. Ashore on Fourth Cliff. Liverpool for Boston. Passengers and general cargo saved.

Jan. 30, 1908. Schooner Helenos. Fernandina to Boston laden with lumber. Total loss.

April 27, 1909. Gypsum Queen. Port Greville for Boston. Saved.
Dec. 26, 1909. Schooner Nantasket. Wrecked on Cedar Point.
Feb. 12, 1910. Schooner Matiana. Ashore on North Scituate Beach.
Sept. 28, 1911. Schooner Island Jack. Boston to Plymouth. Saved.
Aug. 5, 1912. Schooner Edith. Boston to New York. Saved.
Aug. 5, 1912. Schooner Vivian, Boston, cruising. Saved.
Sept. 28, 1914. Barge Jonas H. French. North River to Boston. Lost.
Aug. 3, 1915. Barge Two Bills. Milton to Cape Cod Canal. Saved.
Nov. 3, 1915. Lehigh Valley barge No. 54. For Cohasset (Minot's Light). Saved.

Mar. 3, 1916. Barge Ashland. Boston to Philadelphia. Wrecked on North Scituate Beach. Entire loss.

Mar. 3, 1916. Barge Kohinoor. Boston to Philadelphia. Wrecked on North Scituate Beach. Entire loss with four of crew.

Mar. 5, 1917. Schooner Henry Withington. Bucksport to New York. Total loss.

Aug. 24, 1918. Barge Jacania. On ledge near Minot's Light. Saved.
April 29, 1919. Barque Professor Koch. From South African ports to Boston with a two million dollar cargo of wool and hides, ashore at Scituate Harbor. Saved.

It is but necessary to call attention to the great sacrifice of both life and property evidenced by these records to show the urgent need of the continuance of the work begun in 1878 to create a harbor of refuge at this place. The same conditions which have resulted in the building of the ship canal across the Cape, accentuate the demand for this adjunct —this harbor of refuge—for the protection of shipping which by use of the canal has become necessarily subject to the danger of lee shores in making the distance from the entrance of the canal to Boston.

The following list of the vessels and their tonnage which have sought safety and shelter in stress of weather within the protection of the promontories of Scituate harbor during the last eighteen months appear to be conclusive of this need.

Steamers,	5
Barques	1
Schooners	50
Barges	5
Tugs	16
Dredges	4
Pleasure craft	54
Fishing craft	300
Total number of vessels	435
Total tonnage (estimated)	12,800

II.

AS AN ADJUNCT TO THE CAPE COD SHIP CANAL

The Cape Cod Ship Canal is largely used by tugs and their tows coming from Norfolk, Baltimore and Philadelphia. This tonnage with other classes of shipping appears in the following table prepared by the Marine Department of the Boston Chamber of Commerce.

ARRIVALS FROM DOMESTIC PORTS DURING 1917, WITH GROSS TONNAGE

Class	No.	From Southern Ports Gross Tonnage
Steamers	2,192	5,320,061
Schooners	61	46,906
Tugs	1,358	426,291
Barges	2,577	2,381,750
Totals, 1917	6,188	8,175,008
Totals, 1916	7,225	9,974,884
Totals, 1915	6,893	9,755,147
Totals, 1914	6,269	9,254,776

As to the total of coastwise traffic passing Scituate to and from all ports Prof. Henry R. Johnson of the University of Pennsylvania, testifying in the suit arising out of the condemnation of the Cape Cod Canal in the United States District Court for Massachusetts, stated that for the year ending August 31, 1909, the total number of vessels passing through Pollock Rip Slue was 22,841 and these vessels had a gross tonnage of 26,465,000. During the war this gross tonnage had become reduced to 18,108,893. He estimated an increase of 34,500,000 gross tons in 1933 and 46,200,000 in 1943.

The use to which the canal has already been put has demonstrated that the sea wall built at the mouth of the ditch is inadequate for the purposes of permanent shelter in stress of weather. Captains of these craft coming through the canal must continue their course across the bay, on a treacherous coast, the nearest port, Plymouth, entirely unavailable as a haven. In this aspect, and it has become more apparent as the tonnage passing through the canal has increased, a harbor of refuge must be created.

Scituate naturally presents itself as affording this opportunity. Long before the canal was completed, the project of establishing a harbor of refuge at Scituate was taken up by the National Congress, reported favorably by the Army Engineers, and in 1878 by Act of June 18 of that year, an appropriation was made for a survey with a view to the adaptability of Scituate harbor as a harbor of refuge.

In his report made to the Chief of Engineers, General Humphreys, Lieut.-Col. George Thom has this to say concerning the necessity for the establishment of a harbor of refuge in this locality and the adaptability of Scituate for its location.

"The coast between Scituate and the entrance to Boston Harbor is so densely studded with dangerous shoals and sunken rocks, that no vessel could find shelter there at times when most necessary, in fogs and easterly storms; so that if a vessel passing around Cape Cod, or coming elsewhere from the eastward, should fail to make Boston Harbor and fall to the leeward, it could now find no other refuge except Plymouth Harbor, the approach to which at the 'Cow Yard' is difficult and dangerous, especially to strangers. To provide a harbor of refuge, under these difficulties, that shall be easy of access and afford a safe anchorage for coasters, fishermen, and other vessels that would seek it, is an object much desired by those most interested in the commerce and navigation of this coast."

There was appended to this report "in order to show the importance that is given to the subject of making this a 'harbor of refuge' and the benefit that would thereby result to the navigation and commerce of this coast" a report of the

Barge Ashland ashore on Mike's Ledge, North Scituate two miles from proposed harbor of refuge, on the morning of March 4, 1916 about 10.30 A.M.

Deck house of barge Ashland, with crew of five breaking away from barge which has just begun to founder.   March 4, 1916, 10.45 A.M.

Deck house of barge Ashland in the surf at North Scituate March 4, 1916. Crew is seen by the rail.

Rescue of the crew of the barge Ashland at North Scituate March 4, 1916 by the members of Coast Guard Station 27.

Committee of the Board of Trade of Boston prepared in the summer of 1878. This committee in advocating the establishment of a harbor of refuge at Scituate called the attention of the Engineers to the fact that "during the winter, and in fact for about eight months of the year, the winds are accompanied by thick weather, rain, sleet, or snow, sometimes by all together, and oftentimes by intense cold, rendering it at such times very difficult, if not impossible, to work or manage a vessel, so that, failing to reach Boston harbor, she is virtually at the mercy of the elements and in a situation of the utmost peril."

As a result of this report Congress in 1880 by Act of June 14 of that year started the project with an appropriation of $7500. From thence and in the years following to 1899 when $15,000 was appropriated and expended, approximately $105,000 has been expended. Two breakwaters have been built, dredging has been done in the anchorage basin and in the channel leading to the town wharves. The result of the erection of these breakwaters has been what was apparently not at all contemplated by the Engineers. Instead of scouring out the harbor behind them they have served to create a bar to the eastward which acts as a menace to vessels seeking shelter there in stress of weather.

The improvements which are herein later proposed will remove this menace, prevent a further like accretion and fit the harbor for what it was intended in 1878 that it should become, to wit: an adequate and useful harbor of refuge. In addition to what is already urged, the necessities springing from other considerations are given in the language of Rear Admiral Francis T. Bowles, whose sagacity is seldom questioned. Testifying before Judge Morton in the District Court of the United States for the district of Massachusetts in the condemnation proceedings already mentioned on October 22, 1919, he said:

"Cape Cod, with the shoals and islands about it, forms the greatest and most dangerous obstruction to navigation on the coast of the United States, and perhaps in the world. While there is a saving of distance in going from New York to Boston by the Cape Cod Canal on ordinary courses, amounting to perhaps sixty miles, this saving of distance is not the important feature in reference to traffic and navigation. As some confirmation and illustration of this, there were at Pollock Rip Lightship, from 1909 to 1916 one hundred and twenty-seven days annually of fog or 1096 fog hours. The result of that is that vessels either coming in from the south by Gay Head or coming from the west from New York, wait at Vineyard Haven until the weather clears, or until the wind is more favorable for going round the Cape, on account of the very serious dangers incurred in the Pollock Rip Slue. That creates a very considerable delay and much greater delay on the average than the distance involved.

A committee of the Massachusetts Legislature reported in 1860 that there had been eight hundred and twenty-seven marine disasters about

Cape Cod in the years from 1843 to 1859 with an estimated annual loss of $581,000. The United States Life Saving Service compiled a statement of marine disasters occurring in the twenty-eight years from 1875 to 1903. There were six hundred and eighty-seven wrecks and the property lost amounted to $162,179,615 and the lives lost during that time were one hundred and five. The United States Coast Guard Service has tabulated the wrecks from 1907 to 1917, ten years, which show wrecks of three hundred and twenty-six vessels, the property lost amounting to $1,653,770 and the lives to thirty-two. These wrecks were all in Cape Cod and its immediate vicinity.*

A committee in the year 1790 reported that there were six hundred vessels annually passing from the south to the north of Cape Cod. It gave no idea of the size of these ships and that six hundred, the way it was phrased, would amount to what we call twelve hundred vessels passing the Cape, because I presume those that came from the North went back. The committee of 1860 reported that ten thousand vessels annually pass Cape Cod and estimated the tonnage at two million tons. Brigadier-General William T. Russell, United States Army, on April 4, 1918, in a letter addressed to the Chief of Engineers (Document 1768, Sixty-fifth Congress) stated that 'in normal times there are approximately twenty-five thousand vessels rounding Cape Cod per annum.' There is a consensus of judgment that the gross tonnage of these vessels amounts to twenty-five million tons."

Speaking of the navigation across Massachusetts Bay passing Scituate, and through the Cape Cod Canal in time of war, Admiral Bowles said:

"The other war purposes to which the canal can be put in its present condition: it permits the movement of troops. The movement of a division of troops, a division organized at the present time, would require a very large number of cars upon a railway, I am not prepared to say how many, whether it would be five hundred or a thousand. Our ideas in this respect have been somewhat modified by the recent war. But the movement, the sudden movement of one division of troops would be sufficient to dislocate seriously the operations of the best railroad; whereas those troops could be readily moved without disturbance of any kind by water through the canal with entire safety. The protection of the coast of the United States by fortification is proceeding upon a plan made many years ago and from time to time somewhat modified, but has proceeded very slowly; and there is no doubt that in the event of a prospective war, there would be an enormous activity in the further protection of the coast. The canal would permit the transfer of artillery and ammunition with entire safety. Now, the second feature of the military value of the canal — the preservation of the coasting trade in spite of a blockade. It is not wholly a commercial feature that the ordinary processes of production should continue during war. The great cities of this country are the center of its system of production and the industry of the people. To attack, to paralyze, a great city, is a most effective attack, because paralysis of the Hinterland, the factories and productive elements of the interior, ensues from it. Therefore, during the war it is more essential than ever that the channels of trade should be preserved; and the possibility of continuing the coastwise traffic in spite of an attack by an enemy fleet is equally essential to the life of the nation."

---

* The number does not include those set forth in the other tables of this brief which occurred at Scituate.

Gen. George W. Goethals, the builder of the Panama Canal, who when a colonel of Engineers stationed at Newport, R. I., in 1903 investigated the matter of a canal across Cape Cod and reported to the government as to its availability, testified in the same proceeding. He said:

"In 1902, then being a colonel of Engineers in the United States Army, I was in charge at Newport, R. 1. I have been familiar with the locality of Cape Cod and Massachusetts Bay for many years. From 1886 or 1887 my legal residence has been at Vineyard Haven, Martha's Vineyard and I became more intimately acquainted with the locality by reason of my service in charge of the Engineer district at Newport. Under the River and Harbor Act of June 13, 1902, I was made a member of the board which reported upon the relative merits of certain proposed localities for harbors of refuge at Block Island, Point Judith; in Vineyard and Nantucket Sounds and the east shore of Cape Cod. At that time this board discussed the advisability of a canal across Cape Cod. It is very difficult to get congressmen to read reports, their time is pretty well occupied, and I thought that an illustration of the dangers that the route around the Cape was attended with would be illuminating, and I prepared a tracing (map) locating the wrecks that have occurred there.*

During the time that I was in charge at Newport, it was generally believed that the commerce through this section and around the Cape aggregated some 22,000,000 tons of shipping. In 1908 the gross tonnage reported in the Chief of Engineers' annual report for 1908 is 20,522,948 gross tons. The same report for the fiscal year ending June 30, 1919, gives these numbers of vessels passing around Cape Cod in the years stated:

Year	Number of vessels
1908	19,232
1914	17,238
1915	17,153
1916	17,208
1917	14,111
1918	7,098

these being calendar years. This decrease is accounted for in the fact that the old sailing vessels are diminishing in number.

The Cape Cod canal is regarded as one of the links of the intra-coastal canal system; in the commerce from the Lakes through the New York system of canals, Long Island Sound and New England ports. This because it prevents the break-up of cargo. The barges come right through and go direct to their destination, which would not be possible if they had to take the other route.

It was useful in the last war in transporting ammunition from one side to the other, for the passage of torpedo boats and submarines, and it could also always be of great value for that class of vessels and for the light-draught cruiser and for supply ships. As a military measure it would maintain constantly in use a line for the coastwise trade.

I look for a very large expanse in the trade of the Cape Cod Canal. Shipping (if wrecked) cannot be duplicated rapidly and the coastwise shipping is coming into its own very rapidly. The railroads have got to transfer to the steamships part of the load that they are not now carrying."

*The data given on page   of this brief is in part from this map.

From all of the foregoing it sufficiently appears that the use to which the canal is already being put is an extended one: that as this use increases the necessity for a harbor of refuge at Scituate or some other point between Sandwich and Boston multiplies in the same relative proportion. Present day conditions have caused a return of sentiment to the opinions entertained in 1880 when the harbor of refuge at Scituate was begun. The causes for the abandonment of the project after $100,000 and more had been expended upon it are a part of its history and ought, in any discussion upon the subject, fairly to be set forth so far as can be obtained from the reports made by those whose judgment was required in the determination of discontinuance.

III

FORMER WORK AND APPROPRIATIONS

In 1903 the National Congress had apparently undergone a change of conviction in regard to waterways improvements and constructions in general, and harbors of refuge along the New England coast in particular, from that which it held when it set about creating a harbor of refuge for distressed seafarers, at Scituate. While that retrograde opinion has entirely disappeared in the years succeeding 1903 it was responsible at that time for the discontinuance of appropriations and work upon this project.

The following is from the report of the Chief of Engineers:

1907. In pursuance of a resolution of the Committee on Rivers and Harbors of the House of Representatives, the Board of Engineers for Rivers and Harbors has considered the project for this work, and in its report, published in annual report of the Chief of Engineers for 1903, pages 777-780, concurs in the opinion of the district officer that this place is not worthy of further improvement as a harbor of refuge, but in order to realize the greatest advantage from work already done, recommends the discontinuance of the present project for the improvement of Scituate harbor and the adoption of a project for obtaining a channel six feet deep at mean low water and one hundred feet wide from the entrance to the docks, at the cost of $18,000.

The improvement of the channel has admitted to the wharves barges carrying 700 to 800 tons of coal each, in place of schooners carrying 150 to 200 tons, and is reported to have reduced freight rates fifty to seventy-five cents a ton,

Members of Coast Guard Station 27, North Scituate after rescuing crew of the barge Ashland March 4, 1916.

The captain and crew of the barge Ashland rescued by and cared for at Coast Guard Station 27, North Scituate March 4, 1916.

Wreck of the schooner Helena on the Fourth Cliff, Scituate two miles from proposed harbor of refuge.

Barque Prof. Koch from South American ports to Boston with a cargo valued at $2,000,000 in safety under the lee of the North Breakwater, Scituate Harbor, April 29, 1919.

which it is reported would be further reduced about twenty-five cents a ton if the channel be deepened to six feet, as recommended.

The commerce benefited by this improvement consists of coal and building materials, of which 8623 tons was received in 1903 and 8197 tons in 1906.

The existing project, as reported by a Board of Engineers, September 18, 1880, with map of the harbor, is published in annual report of the Chief of Engineers for 1881, page 523.

Amount (estimated) required for completion of existing project, $186,500.

IMPROVEMENT OF HARBOR AT SCITUATE, MASSACHUSETTS

For want of funds no work has been done upon this improvement during the fiscal year ending June 30, 1907.

Money Statement

Amount (estimated) required for completion of existing project $186,500
Amount that can be profitably expended in fiscal year ending
   June 30, 1909, for work of improvement.................. 18,000

Submitted in compliance with requirements of sundry civil acts of June 4, 1897.

Appropriations

March 2, 1829...	$180
August 30, 1852..	1,000
June 14, 1880...	7,500
March 3, 1881...	10,000
August 2, 1882..	10,000
July 5, 1884..	10,000
August 5, 1886..	10,000
August 11, 1888.......................................	5,000
September 19, 1890....................................	10,000
July 13, 1892...	10,000
August 18, 1894.......................................	10,000
June 3, 1896..	6,000
March 3, 1899...	15,000
Total (b)..	$104,680

Commercial Statistics

Articles	1904 Tons	1905 Tons	1906 Tons
Coal..	5200	4605	3951
Lumber and shingles.......................	5000	2872	3768
Bricks......................................	600	395	375
Lime..	350	137	103
Sand..	180	...	...
Total	11,330	8009	8197

(a) Allotment from appropriation for Boston harbor, to which appropriation $683.42 was restored.

(b) From 1831 to 1858 inclusive $89.02 were carried to the surplus fund.

14. Harbor at Scituate, Mass.—In its original condition the depth on the bar was about two and one-half feet at mean low water, and the entrance was obstructed by many sunken bowlders; of the low-water area of about fifty-seven acres, six acres had a depth of at least three feet at mean low water, and there was little protection against the sea.

The original project seems to have been to protect the beach between Cedar Point and the mainland on the northerly side of the entrance to the harbor, upon which, prior to operations under the existing project (in 1829 to 1852), $1,090.98 was expended in building 450 linear feet of brush and stone bulkhead and 385 linear feet of stone apron ten feet wide.

The existing project adopted by the act of June 14, 1880, is to build, of rubblestone, a north breakwater 800 feet and a south breakwater 730 feet long, to dredge an anchorage basin of 30 acres and an entrance channel 2700 feet long and 300 feet wide, with depths at mean low water of 15 feet at the entrance, 12 to 15 feet between the breakwaters, 12 feet immediately back of the south breakwater, 10 feet in the anchorage basin and 3 feet in the channel to the wharves, at an estimated cost of $100,000 for the breakwaters and of $190,000 for the dredging; total, $290,000.

Up to the close of the fiscal year ending June 30, 1908, there had been expended on the work under the existing project $103,500. Of this amount about $56,000 was expended for dredging, including about $9500 expended from 1899 to 1901 in maintenance of the dredged channel. The amount previously expended for maintenance is not ascertainable.

With that expenditure all known bowlders obstructing the entrance to the harbor have been removed; the anchorage basin, 350 feet by 400 feet, has been dredged 7 feet at mean low water, and the channel from the sea to the basin has been dredged 7 feet deep, 100 feet wide, 1600 feet long; the channel, 2150 feet long from the anchorage basin to the town wharves, has been dredged 3 feet at mean low water at least 100 feet wide; and 720 linear feet of the north breakwater and 450 linear feet of the south breakwater have been built.

Fifty per cent of breakwater construction and 21 per cent of the dredging authorized have been completed.

Through deterioration of the dredged channel, as reported by local interests, the channel depth has been reduced to less than 2 feet at mean low water. The mean range of tides is 9.8 feet.

The commerce benefited by this improvement consists of coal and building materials, of which about 15,000 tons was carried in 1902 and 8087 tons in 1907. In 1883, prior to any dredging by the United States, the value of the annual commerce was reported to be $677,837, which had in 1907 declined to less than one-tenth of that sum.

In pursuance of a resolution of the Committee on Rivers and Harbors of the House of Representatives, the Board of Engineers for Rivers and Harbors in 1903 considered the project for this work, and in its report published in the annual report of the Chief of Engineers for that year, pages 777-780, concurred in the opinion of the district officer that this place is not worthy of further improvement as a harbor of refuge, but in order to realize the greatest advantage from work already done, recommended the discontinuance of the present project for the improvement of Scituate harbor and the adoption of a project for obtaining a channel 6 feet deep at mean low water and 100 feet wide from the entrance to the docks at the cost of $18,000.

No appropriations have been made for this work for nine years past, and the district officer has reported that, by reason of the diminution in water-borne commerce, and the scarcity of light-draft vessels suitable for the authorized depth, the public benefits to be anticipated are entirely disproportionate to the cost of completing the improvement and the excessive cost of maintaining it. For these reasons no further estimate for the improvement of the harbor is submitted.

The existing project, as reported by a Board of Engineers September 18, 1880, with map of the harbor, is published in annual report of the Chief of Engineers for 1881, page 523.

Amount (estimated) required for completion of existing project, $186,500.00.

(See Appendix B-14).

IV

SUBSTANTIAL WORK HAS ALREADY BEEN DONE IT IS AVAILABLE FOR PRESENT USE

It is believed by these proponents that an addition to the present northerly breakwater extending from its southerly end southeasterly for a distance of five hundred feet and of an equal width with the structure already built, will, with additional dredging at the mouth of and within the harbor accomplish the result recommended by the Engineers forty years ago and now brought into prominent need by the use of the Cape Cod Canal. As the means of making the structure already built useful and available for a continuation and final accomplishment of the work, are a matter of engineering, we do not presume to offer suggestion in this regard other than to say that material from the quarries of both Rockport and Quincy is readily at hand through cheap water transportation for delivery at Scituate.

V

THE COMMERCIAL IMPORTANCE OF THE PROJECT

As is shown in the report of the Chief of Engineers the commerce benefited by the improvements of the harbor already made consists of coal and building materials. The amounts appear in the table accompanying the report for the years 1904, 1905 and 1906. In the thirteen years which have elapsed since those statistics were prepared the harbor has increased in commercial importance. Since then the Boston Sand and Gravel Company has engaged in extensive operations for the removal of near by cliffs containing a high-grade merchantable sand and gravel and is now marketing that commodity.

The rapid and permanent growth of the town as a place for summer residence has increased the consumption of coal and building materials to an extent which is shown in the following tables:

TABLE SHOWING MATERIALS RECEIVED AND ENTERED AT SCITUATE

1905, Total net tons, all material, 8,009

1918, Total net tons, all material, 12,800

1910, Coal, 4372 net tons,
Lumber, 1,526,773 feet,
Brick, 59,300,
Lime, 1079 barrels.
Shingles, 3,195,000
Clapboards 5000,

Total gross tonnage of shipping engaged in transportation of this material, (estimated), 9000.

1911, Total net tons, all material 11,977,

1914, Coal, 8375 net tons,
Lumber, 1,131,892 feet,
Brick, 256,100,
Lime, 603 barrels,
Laths, 279,900,
Shingles, 3,865,000
Oak piling, 4 cargoes in barges.

This material was carried in 22 bottoms (11 barges and 11 schooners) with a total gross tonnage of 12,650.

Wreck of the schooner Nantasket at Scituate, a gun shot from the entrance of the proposed harbor of refuge, December 26, 1909. The life saving crew is seen rescuing the crew in the breeches buoy.

Damage done at the Third Cliff, North Scituate, one mile from proposed harbor of refuge by the storm of December 26, 1909.

1915,   Coal 8853 net tons,
Lumber, 1,124,512 feet
Brick, 283,100
Laths. 693,000
Shingles, 1,450,000.
Lime, 1,030 barrels.
Screenings, 117 tons.
Wharf lumber, 20,000 feet.

This material was carried in 24 bottoms (13 barges and 11 schooners) with a total gross tonnage of 14,650.

The last appropriation made by Congress in 1909 (to wit, $15,000 after the project of creating a harbor of refuge had been abandoned) was appropriated and expended upon the facts found and determined that the harbor was one of sufficient commercial importance to warrant this outlay.

The diminution in water-borne commerce reaching this port is due to the fact that the depth and width of the channel are both insufficient to accommodate the draft of vessels now engaged in transporting that commerce.

With the appropriation by the Federal government of the sum of $186,000 (reported by the Engineers as necessary to complete the dredging of an adequate anchorage basin and channel) the coal for instance which is now brought all-rail to Scituate would come by water with an advantage to the consumer of a reduced freight rate from fifty to seventy-five cents a ton and a consequent corollary benefit to the coast-wise shipping which the post-bellum policy of the government seeks to encourage and build up.

The public benefits to be derived, therefore, from a purely commercial standpoint, warrant the expenditure of a sum totalling two hundred thousand dollars. This would seem to be adequate to not only provide the harbor of refuge but to afford the town and the contiguous inland municipalities which trade with and are dependent upon it, the benefit of maritime rates to which its geographical location entitles it.

Respectfully submitted,

HARVEY H. PRATT,
For Scituate Harbor Improvement Committee.

APPENDIX B-14

IMPROVEMENT OF HARBOR AT SCITUATE, MASSACHUSETTS

For want of funds no work has been done upon this improvement during the fiscal year ending June 30, 1908.

MONEY STATEMENT

Amount (estimated) required for completion of existing project $186,500.

APPROPRIATIONS

March 2, 1829	$180
August 30, 1852	1,000
June 14, 1880	7,500
March 3, 1881	10,000
August 2, 1882	10,000
July 5, 1884	10,000
August 5, 1886	10,000
August 11, 1888	5,000
September 19, 1890	10,000
July 13, 1892	10,000
August 18, 1894	10,000
June 3, 1896	6,000
March 3, 1899	15,000
Total(a)	$104,680

COMMERCIAL STATISTICS

Articles	1905 Tons	1906 Tons	1907 Tons
Coal	4605	3951	5634
Lumber and shingles	2872	3768	2161
Brick	395	375	234
Lime	137	103	58
	8009	8197	8087

Commerce is carried on in light-draft vessels and in barges of 1000 tons capacity, drawing 13½ feet loaded. The latter owing to insufficient channel depth, are unable to bring in more than 700 tons in a cargo with proportionate increase in cost of transportation.

(a) From 1831 to 1858, inclusive, $89.02 were carried to the surplus fund.